LIGHTNING
BOLT
BOOKS™

Meet a Baby Wombat

Jon M. Fishman

Lerner Publications ◆ Minneapolis

Lerner Publications Company
A division of Lerner Publishing Group, Inc.
241 First Avenue North
Minneapolis, MN 55401 USA

For reading levels and more information, look up this title at www.lernerbooks.com.

Library of Congress Cataloging-in-Publication Data

Names: Fishman, Jon M., author.
Title: Meet a baby wombat / Jon M. Fishman.
Description: Minneapolis : Lerner Publications, 2017. | Series: Lightning bolt books. Baby Australian animals | Includes bibliographical references and index. | Audience: Ages 6 to 9. | Audience: Grades K to 3.
Identifiers: LCCN 2016038213 (print) | LCCN 2016053868 (ebook) | ISBN 9781512433876 (lb : alk. paper) | ISBN 9781512450590 (eb pdf)
Subjects: LCSH: Wombats—InfancyJuvenile literature. | Wombats—Life cycles—Juvenile literature.
Classification: LCC QL737.M39 F57 2017 (print) | LCC QL737.M39 (ebook) | DDC 599.2/4—dc23

LC record available at https://lccn.loc.gov/2016038213

Manufactured in the United States of America
1-42023-23893-11/4/2016

Table of Contents

Pouch Life

A baby common wombat will be born soon. It has been growing inside its mother for about twenty-one days. A baby wombat is called a joey.

Common wombats are just one kind of wombat. There are two other kinds too!

The joey looks like a pink jelly bean. It has no hair. It can't see or hear.

The newborn joey cannot protect itself. It needs its mother to keep it safe.

A newborn joey weighs less than 2 grams (0.07 ounces). That is about the weight of a small paper clip.

The joey crawls to its mother's pouch as soon as it is born. Inside the pouch are two teats. The joey drinks milk from one of the teats.

The joey grows quickly in its mother's pouch. It begins to see and hear.

Time to Grow

A wombat mother's pouch faces backward. The pouch opening faces the same direction as the mother's bottom. That helps keep dirt out of the pouch when she digs.

This joey is looking out from its mother's pouch.

The joey stays in the pouch for about eight months. Then it starts exploring outside the pouch.

Joeys weigh around 7 pounds (3 kilograms) at this age. A newborn human weighs about the same.

The joey is still not fully grown. But it has fur.

Huh-huh. The mother calls to her joey. The joey responds. The mother stays close while the joey explores.

A mother and her joey make noises for safety. Hearing the noises helps them stay close to each other.

Plant Food

Joeys drink milk even after they come out of the pouch. They also begin to eat grass.

This joey is staying safe in its burrow.

A joey may stay behind at night while its mother finds food. The joey will wait in a burrow.

Joeys follow their mother at night when they get a little older. The wombats graze on grass.

Wombats also eat other plants.

Wombats have special teeth for eating grass. Chewing on grass can rub away at a wombat's teeth. The teeth keep growing so the wombat can keep eating.

A New Start

A joey stops drinking milk when it is twelve to fifteen months old. It usually stays with its mother for another few months. Then it sets off on its own.

Wombats live in burrows. They dig burrows in the ground.

Wombats reach full size at about two years of age. They can weigh 50 to 90 pounds (23 to 41 kg). That's about the weight of a large dog.

A wombat is usually ready to mate when it is two years old. A female wombat has one joey every two or three years.

Wombats in the wild live alone. They live for up to fifteen years.

Wombat Life Cycle

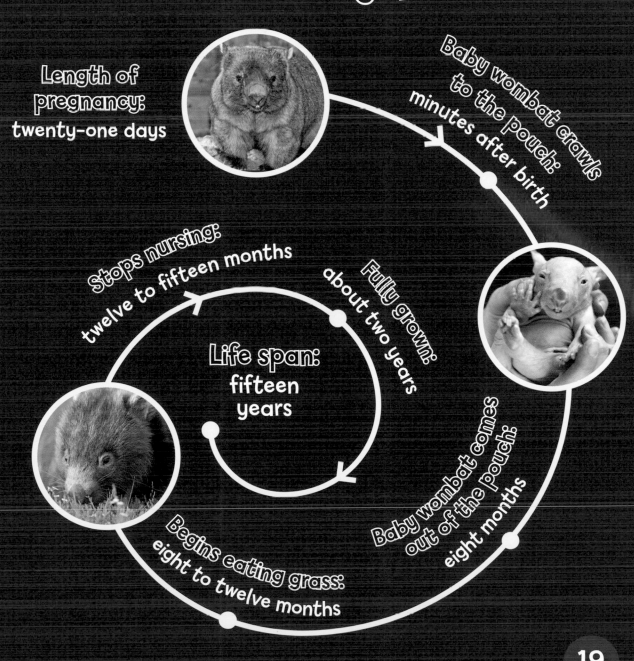

Length of pregnancy: twenty-one days

Baby wombat crawls to the pouch: minutes after birth

Stops nursing: twelve to fifteen months

Fully grown: about two years

Life span: fifteen years

Baby wombat comes out of the pouch: eight months

Begins eating grass: eight to twelve months

Habitat in Focus

- Wild wombats live only in Australia. Australia's habitat has many interesting animals such as koalas and kangaroos.

- Wombats spend most of the day in their burrows. They come out at night when it is cooler. That way, they will not get so hot while trying to find food.

- A wombat may have as many as ten burrows. The burrows are lined with leaves, grass, and twigs.

Fun Facts

- Joeys often play. They jump and roll around. They run off and then hurry back to their mother.

- The oldest known wombat is named Patrick. He lives at a park in Australia. Patrick the wombat turned thirty-one in August 2016.

- Wombats have strong legs for digging. Their strength also helps them run fast. They can race up to 25 miles (40 kilometers) per hour.

Glossary

burrow: a hole an animal digs to live in

graze: to eat plants

joey: a baby wombat

mate: join together to produce young

newborn: a baby that was just born

teat: the place on a female wombat's body where the joey drinks milk

Further Reading

Animal Fact Guide: Common Wombat
http://www.animalfactguide.com/animal-facts/common-wombat

Discovery Kids: Australia Zoo
http://discoverykids.com/games/australia-zoo

Fishman, Jon M. *Meet a Baby Koala*. Minneapolis: Lerner Publications, 2018.

Owings, Lisa. *Learning about Australia*. Minneapolis: Lerner Publications, 2016.

Phillips, Dee. *Wombat's Burrow*. New York: Bearport, 2014.

San Diego Zoo Kids: Wombat
http://animals.sandiegozoo.org/animals/wombat

Index

Photo Acknowledgments

The images in this book are used with the permission of: © iStockphoto.com/wrangel, p. 2; © iStockphoto.com/marco3t, p. 4; Gerhard Koertner/NHPA/Photoshot/Newscom, p. 5; © Alex Kosev/Shutterstock.com, p. 6; © Darroch Donald/Alamy, p. 7; © iStockphoto.com/ Boyshots, p. 8; © Dave Watts/Alamy, p. 9; © Gerry Pearce/imageBROKER/Alamy, pp. 10, 22; © NULL/FLPA/Alamy, p. 11; © Jurgen and Christine Sohns/Minden Pictures, p. 12; © Jim Zuckerman/Alamy, p. 13; © Simon Anders/Alamy, p. 14; © Sidney Smith/Minden Pictures, p. 15; © David Hosking/Alamy, p. 16; © Sean Crane/Minden Pictures, p. 17; © Mark Newman/ Minden Pictures, p. 18; © iStockphoto.com/lonewolfshome, p. 19 (adult wombat); © GREG WOOD/AFP/Getty Images, p. 19 (hairless joey); Jürgen & Christine Sohns/imageBROKER/ Newscom, p. 19 (wombat eating grass); © iStockphoto.com/bennymarty, p. 20.

Front cover: © Newspix/Getty Images, front cover.

Main body text set in Billy Infant regular 28/36. Typeface provided by SparkType.